D1228548

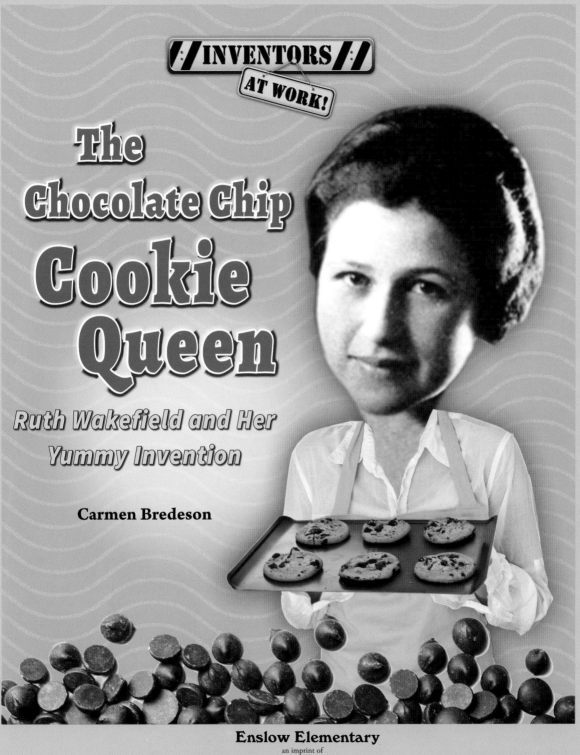

//INVENTORS// AT WORK!

The Chocolate Chip Cookie Queen

Ruth Wakefield and Her Yummy Invention

Carmen Bredeson

Enslow Elementary

an imprint of

 Enslow Publishers, Inc.
40 Industrial Road
Box 398
Berkeley Heights, NJ 07922
USA

http://www.enslow.com

Enslow Elementary, an imprint of Enslow Publishers, Inc.

Enslow Elementary® is a registered trademark of Enslow Publishers, Inc.

Copyright © 2014 by Carmen Bredeson

All rights reserved.

No part of this book may be reproduced by any means without the written permission of the publisher.

Library of Congress Cataloging-in-Publication Data

Bredeson, Carmen.
  The chocolate chip cookie queen : Ruth Wakefield and her yummy invention / Carmen Bredeson.
  pages cm. — (Inventors at work!)
  Includes index.
  Summary: "A biography of Ruth Wakefield's life, and her invention of the chocolate chip cookie"—Provided by publisher.
  ISBN 978-0-7660-4242-1
  1. Wakefield, Ruth Graves—Juvenile literature. 2. Cooks—United States—Biography—Juvenile literature.
    3. Women cooks—United States—Biography—Juvenile literature. 4. Chocolate chip cookies—History—Juvenile literature. I. Title.
  TX649.W33B74 2014
  641.5092—dc23
  [B]
                                          2013008770

Future editions:
Paperback ISBN: 978-1-4644-0427-6
EPUB ISBN: 978-1-4645-1233-9
Single-User ISBN: 978-1-4646-1233-6
Multi-User ISBN: 978-0-7660-5865-1

Printed in the United States of America
102013 Lake Book Manufacturing, Inc., Melrose Park, IL
10 9 8 7 6 5 4 3 2 1

To Our Readers: We have done our best to make sure all Internet Addresses in this book were active and appropriate when we went to press. However, the author and the publisher have no control over and assume no liability for the material available on those Internet sites or on other Web sites they may link to. Any comments or suggestions can be sent by e-mail to comments@enslow.com or to the address on the back cover.

♻ Enslow Publishers, Inc., is committed to printing our books on recycled paper. The paper in every book contains 10% to 30% post-consumer waste (PCW). The cover board on the outside of each book contains 100% PCW. Our goal is to do our part to help young people and the environment too!

Photo Credits: Courtesy Framingham State University Archives, pp. 16, 21; Courtesy King Arthur Flour, pp. 10, 30; Courtesy Massachusetts State Archives, p. 38; Easton Historical Society, Massachusetts, pp. 12, 15; Jupiterimages/Photos.com, p. 4; National Archives, p. 35; Shutterstock.com, pp. 13, 14, 26, 40, 41, 42, 43, 44; Stonehill College Archives and Historical Collections: Stanley A. Bauman Photograph, pp. 6, 18, 23, 25, 28, 29, 37; This photo is made available as a courtesy by Nestle USA, pp. 8, 32.

Cover Photo: Portrait: Courtesy Framingham State University Archives; Clipart: Shutterstock.com.

CONTENTS

Inventing a Cookie

SMILE if you like COOKIES! How about a warm, fresh-from-the-oven sugar cookie? Maybe a nice, chewy oatmeal raisin cookie? Or do you prefer the sweet taste of a homemade chocolate chip cookie? If so, you are not alone. More than half of the cookies baked at home are chocolate chip. It is the most popular cookie in the United States.

Did you know that before the 1930s, this kind of cookie didn't exist? That's right. There were no chocolate chip cookies. There were not even any chocolate chips. They had not been invented yet. So who thought up this yummy cookie?

Ruth and her daughter, Mary Jane, bake a batch of cookies.

We have Ruth Graves Wakefield to thank. She and her husband Kenneth owned a restaurant in Whitman, Massachusetts. It was called the Toll House Inn.

One day, Wakefield was busy in the kitchen. She was mixing up the dough for a batch of her famous Butter Drop Do cookies. She just needed to add some baking chocolate. Where was the baking chocolate? Oh no! It was all gone. There wasn't time to get more before the Inn opened for lunch. Ruth had a problem! But sometimes a problem can lead to a great discovery.

A New Cookie!

Wakefield saw some Nestlé semi-sweet candy bars on the shelf. They would have to do. She used an ice pick to chop the candy into small pieces. Then she stirred the pieces into the dough. She scooped little piles of dough onto the cookie sheets. Into the oven they went. Ten minutes later, she took the cookie sheets out of the oven.

The original chocolate that Ruth Wakefield used for her cookies was a solid candy bar. She broke it into pieces and added it to the dough.

(*This photo is made available as a courtesy by Nestle USA.*)

Ruth Wakefield had thought the chocolate would melt. Instead, the chunks kept their shape. The cookies were ruined. Nobody wanted to eat cookies with hard chunks of chocolate in them. Wakefield was about to toss everything into the trash. Then somebody tasted one of the cookies.

Delicious!

The chocolate wasn't hard. It was soft and gooey and wonderful. More tasting led to more "yummm" sounds. The cookies were a big hit that day. Diners loved them and told their friends. Soon demand for the unique cookies grew. Everybody wanted to try some. Ruth Wakefield called them Toll House Chocolate Crunch Cookies.

Toll House
Chocolate Crunch Cookies

Cream
1 cup butter, add
¾ cup brown sugar
¾ cup granulated sugar and
2 eggs beaten whole. Dissolve
1 tsp. soda in
1 tsp. hot water, and mix
    alternately with
2¼ cups flour sifted with

1 tsp. salt. Lastly add
1 cup chopped nuts and
2 bars (7-oz.) Nestles yellow label chocolate, semi-sweet, which has been cut in pieces the size of a pea.
Flavor with
1 tsp. vanilla and drop half teaspoons on a greased cookie sheet. Bake 10 to 12 minutes in 375° oven. Makes 100 cookies.

Ruth Wakefield's recipe for her original Toll House Chocolate Crunch Cookies

Growing Up

Ruth Graves was born on June 17, 1903, in Easton, Massachusetts. Later Ruth and her mother moved to North Easton. They lived with her mother's parents. Ruth's house was just two blocks from Main Street. The neighborhood had a lot of families. Ruth did not have any brothers or sisters, but there were many children on the block for her to play with.

Ruth's mother and grandmother were both good cooks. Ruth helped in the kitchen when she was just a little girl. Her grandmother taught her to cook many things. There was only one thing her grandmother didn't like. Ruth would use a lot of

Ruth Wakefield grew up in this home in North Easton, Massachusetts.

pots and pans. There was always a big mess to clean up after she cooked.

Ring-Tum-Diddy was one dish the whole family liked. Ruth helped make the melted cheese sauce in a pan. Then she poured the cheese over pieces of toast.

Time for Dessert

Ruth's grandmother made delicious cakes and cookies. One of her best desserts was Applesauce Cake. She didn't use a measuring cup or teaspoons when she cooked. She just scooped a little of this and a pinch of that. Sugar was measured in a blue cup. Flour was measured in a yellow bowl.

Later Ruth owned her own restaurant. She used many of her grandmother's recipes. She had to figure out how to get the amounts just right. She no longer had the blue cup and yellow bowl. She didn't know exactly how big each one was.

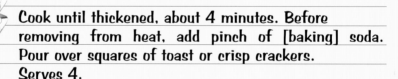

Ring-Tum-Diddy

Melt:	2 tablespoons butter in the top of a double boiler [Be sure to ask an adult to help with the hot pan.]
Blend in:	1 tablespoon flour
Add:	1 cup tomato soup
	1 teaspoon salt
	1 teaspoon Worcestershire sauce
	2 cups finely cut cheese. Stir until melted.
Add:	1 egg, beaten

Cook until thickened, about 4 minutes. Before removing from heat, add pinch of [baking] soda. Pour over squares of toast or crisp crackers. Serves 4.

th Easton, Mass. Oliver Ames High School.

Ruth went to high school here in North Easton, Massachusetts.

School Days

Ruth went to elementary school and high school in North Easton. She graduated from high school in 1920. Then she went to Framingham State Normal School. She wanted to learn more about food. Her grandmother and mother had taught her a lot about cooking. Now she planned to study the science of nutrition.

Ruth graduated from college in 1924. Her yearbook describes her as someone who "accomplishes what she sets out to do!"

Nutrition is the study of how the human body uses food. Which foods are best for good health? Which foods are not as good for our bodies? Ruth learned about vitamins and minerals in the foods we eat. She took all of the classes for her degree in Household Arts. She graduated in 1924.

After graduation, Ruth Graves was a teacher for two years. She taught home economics at Brockton High School. Her students learned about nutrition. They also learned how to shop for food and cook good meals.

Ruth Meets Kenneth

While she was teaching at Brockton, Ruth Graves met Kenneth Wakefield. Kenneth worked in the food industry also. He worked on a ship. He helped plan menus and buy food for each cruise. He also did some of the cooking and other work in the ship's kitchen.

Ruth and Kenneth had a lot in common. Both of them were interested in food and nutrition. The young

Ruth Graves and Kenneth Wakefield were married in 1926. This photo includes their daughter, Mary Jane.

couple fell in love. Ruth had the summer off from school. It was the perfect time for the two to marry. Ruth Graves and Kenneth Wakefield were married on June 26, 1926.

Ruth Wakefield left her teaching job. She took a job with the Brockton Hospital. Ruth worked as a dietician. This is a person who plans menus for the patients in the hospital. Eating healthy food is important for people who are sick. Good food helps people get well faster. Ruth worked with the doctors to plan the best menu for each patient. She made sure the patients got the right food to make them stronger.

A Dream Comes True

Ruth and Kenneth Wakefield had a secret dream. They wanted to own a restaurant. Ruth Wakefield said, "For four years my husband . . . and I dreamed of the kind of eating place we would like to have." They began looking for the right kind of building. Finally they found the perfect place. They scraped together all of their money and bought a small house in Whitman, Massachusetts. It was a very old house, built in 1709. Long ago, it had been a toll house.

In the early days of America, people had to pay to use some roads. The money collected was called a toll. This house was a place where people stopped to pay their tolls. They could also rest and get

Ruth and Kenneth Wakefield bought the Toll House Inn in 1930.

something to eat. While they ate, their horses got food and water in the barn.

The Wakefield's toll house was small, but it was perfect for a little restaurant. The young couple did a lot of work on the house. They painted and cleaned. Then they planned the menu and stocked the kitchen.

The Toll House Inn

In 1930, Ruth and Kenneth opened the Toll House Inn. It had just seven tables. They could only serve thirty-five people at a time. In the beginning, Ruth did most of the cooking. She was also in charge of planning the menus. The Inn became popular very fast. Soon more help was hired to cook and serve. Ruth did not have to cook all the time. Now she could be the hostess and greet the guests. Ruth had a very friendly personality. She made the guests feel right at home. Kenneth ran the kitchen. He made sure that each dish was cooked right.

The dining room was full of antique furniture. Each table was set with a different kind of china and glasses. No two tables were exactly the same. The Toll House Inn was a lovely place to eat. The prices were not too high either. Soon word spread. More and more people arrived. They wanted to try the delicious food at the Toll House Inn. They especially wanted to try the famous cookies.

The Toll House Inn's dining room was filled with tables.
Each table was set with different dishes and glasses.

The Inn Gets Bigger

As the crowds got bigger, the building had to grow. Rooms were added. The original seven tables grew to twenty, forty, then sixty tables. Eventually there were ninety tables that served between 1,000 and 2,000 guests a day. Kenneth and Ruth did not want more than ninety tables. They wanted the Inn to feel warm and cozy. The homey smell of fresh baked bread was always in the air.

It took a lot of people to run such a big restaurant. More than one hundred people worked at the Inn. Some were cooks in the kitchen. Others waited on the tables and brought food to the guests. The waitresses were all young women. They wore

Waitresses at the Toll House Inn wore crisp white blouses and flowered skirts.

flower print skirts, white blouses, and white shoes. The waitresses could not write down any of the orders. They had to remember them. It was hard at first, but they learned to memorize the orders.

Cake or Frosting?

Ruth and Kenneth Wakefield had two children, Mary Jane and Don. One of the Inn's desserts was Mary Jane Gingerbread. It was a recipe that Wakefield made with her grandmother, who was also named Mary Jane.

One of the most popular items on the menu was Toll House French Onion Soup. Ruth and Kenneth learned to make this soup on a trip to France one year. They often traveled in the winter. This was when business at the Inn was slower. They liked to try food in other countries. Sometimes they brought back recipes to serve at the Inn.

The Toll House Inn also served a lot of lobster. There were stuffed lobsters, cucumber and lobster sandwiches, and lobster stew. They served two or three TONS of lobster a week! And the lobster was very fresh. It had been in the ocean just an hour before it was delivered to the kitchen.

The Inn was famous for its desserts. There were wonderful cakes on the menu. Don liked the frosting best. His dad liked the cake the most. Mary Jane and her mother liked both the cake and the frosting.

Cookies for All

On Thanksgiving and Christmas, the Inn served whole turkey dinners to the guests. After the meal, the leftovers were boxed up to take home. Wakefield wanted everyone to have turkey and dressing to eat the next day. That is part of the fun of holiday dinners—delicious leftovers.

She also sent along some of her famous Toll House Chocolate Crunch Cookies. Everybody who ate at the Inn got free cookies to take home. There was a small gift shop in the restaurant. Boxes of Toll House Cookies were for sale there also.

Santa and Ruth Wakefield enjoy the holiday party at the Toll House Inn.

Chocolate Chips!

People liked Chocolate Crunch Cookies so much. They started asking for the recipe. Wakefield gladly shared it with her customers. She liked sharing her recipes. Not long after she opened the Inn, Wakefield published a cookbook: *Toll House Tried and True Recipes.* The book had recipes for many of the Inn's most popular dishes. One recipe was for her famous Chocolate Crunch Cookies.

The Toll House Inn holiday dessert table was always filled with Toll House Cookies!

Toll House Tried and True Recipes was filled with recipes of the Inn's most popular dishes.

Wakefield's recipe was also printed in one of the Boston newspapers. Soon everybody was making the cookies. The Nestlé Company noticed that candy bar sales went up. They couldn't figure out why so many people were buying semi-sweet candy bars. Then they heard about Wakefield's cookies and had their answer.

real fact!

Cookies Around the World

The word cookie comes from the Dutch word *koekje*. This means "little cake." In the past, people cooked on wood stoves. The temperature in wood burning stoves was hard to control. Nobody wanted to ruin a whole cake. To test the oven, a small amount of batter was put on a pan in the oven. The cook watched to see how fast it cooked. Then she knew when the oven was hot enough. These little bits of batter were called small cakes. Later they were called cookies. In England and Australia, cookies are called biscuits. In Italy, they are biscotti.

The Nestlé Company made bags of little chocolate bits and had the Toll House Cookie recipe on the bag. (*This photo is made available as a courtesy by Nestle USA.*)

Andrew Nestlé got in touch with Ruth Wakefield. He asked whether they could print her recipe on the back of the candy bar wrapper. She made a deal with them. They could print her recipe. But they had to give her free chocolate bars in return—FOR LIFE! It was a good deal for everyone. Nestlé sold a zillion candy bars and Wakefield got free chocolate for her cookies.

The bars were solid chocolate. They were kind of hard to break up. Nestlé started making lines in the chocolate. The bars were easier to break along the lines. Today's candy bars also have lines so they break into sections.

The Beginning of the Chocolate Chip

Nestlé also sold a small tool. It was used for breaking up the candy into small bits. Then, in 1939, somebody at Nestlé had a bright idea. Why not sell bags of little chocolate bits? That was the beginning of the chocolate chip. The cookie recipe changed a little after that. The candy bars did not have to be broken up. Chocolate chips were added to the dough instead. The name of the cookie changed too. Now it was called Nestlé's Toll House Chocolate Chip Cookie. The recipe for Toll House Cookies is still on every bag of Nestlé chocolate chips.

December 8, 1941—War Begins

Eleven years after the Toll House Inn opened, America entered World War II. Thousands of American soldiers were sent overseas to fight. Many of the soldiers were lonely for home. Ruth and Kenneth wanted to help a little. They sent thousands of boxes of Toll House Cookies to the troops. Cookies were sent until the end of the war. The soldiers got a little taste of home from the Toll House Inn.

Ruth Wakefield mailed her cookies to American troops overseas. They were able to enjoy a taste of home while they fought during World War II.

World War II ended in 1945. Some of the soldiers came to the Inn to eat. One of them was John F. Kennedy. He became a senator and later president of the United States. During all of those years, Kennedy came back to the Inn to enjoy the good food.

Retirement

In 1966, Ruth and Kenneth Wakefield decided to retire. They had owned the Toll House Inn for thirty-six years. Owning a restaurant is a big job. Both of the Wakefields were busy from the time the doors opened until they closed late at night. It was time for a rest. They sold the Toll House Inn in 1966. After she retired, Ruth Wakefield donated many of her cookbooks to Framingham College.

The Rest of the Story

Ruth Graves Wakefield died on January 10, 1977. She gave the world a delicious treat that we still enjoy. On July 9, 1997, the State of Massachusetts made the

The Wakefield family waves from the door of the Toll House Inn.

On July 9, 1997, Massachusetts Governor William Weld made the chocolate chip cookie its official state cookie. The third grade students who thought of the idea look on.

chocolate chip cookie its official state cookie. Later that year, Easton had a Toll House Cookie celebration. There was a parade through town. The parade watchers got cookies and milk. It helped them remember Ruth Wakefield's delicious invention. Why don't you have a chocolate chip cookie in honor of Ruth Wakefield? I bet you can't eat just one.

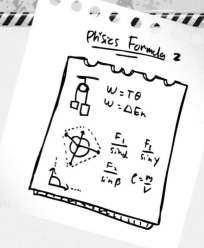

So you want to be an inventor? You can do it! First, you need a terrific idea.

Got a Problem? No Problem!

Many inventions begin when someone thinks of a great solution to a problem. One cold day in 1994, ten-year-old K. K. Gregory was building a snow fort. Soon, she had snow between her mittens and her coat sleeve. Her wrists were cold and wet. She found some scraps of fabric around the house, and used them to make a tube that would fit around her wrist. She cut a thumb hole in the tube to make a kind of fingerless glove, and called it a "Wristie." Wearing mittens over her new invention, her wrists stayed nice and warm when she played outside. Today, the Wristie business is booming.

Now it's your turn. Maybe, like K. K. Gregory, you have an idea for something new that would make your life better or easier. Perhaps you can think of a way to improve an everyday item. Twelve-year-old Becky Schroeder became one of the youngest people ever to receive a U.S. patent after she invented a glow-in-the-dark clipboard that allowed people to write in the dark. Do you like to play sports or board games? James Naismith, inspired by a game he used to play as a boy, invented a new game he called basketball.

Let your imagination run wild. You never know where it will take you.

Research It!

Okay, you have a terrific idea for an invention. Now what do you do?

First, you'll want to make sure that nobody else has

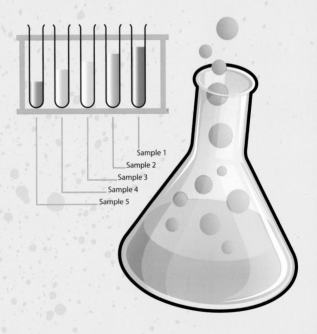

Sample 1
Sample 2
Sample 3
Sample 4
Sample 5

thought of your idea. You wouldn't want to spend hours developing your new invention, only to find that someone else beat you to it. Check out Google Patents (see Learn More for the Web site address), which can help you find out whether your idea is original.

Bring It to Life!

If no one else has thought of your idea, congratulations! Write it down in a notebook. Date and initial every entry you make. If you file a patent for your invention later, this will help you prove that you were the first to think of it. The most important thing about this logbook is that pages cannot be added or subtracted. You can buy a bound notebook at any office supply store.

Draw several different pictures of your invention in your logbook. Try sketching views from above, below, and to the side. Show how big each part of your invention should be.

Build a model. Don't be discouraged if it doesn't work at first. You may have to experiment with different designs and materials. That's part of the fun! Take pictures of everything, and tape them into your logbook. Try your invention out on your friends and family. If they have any suggestions to make it better, build another model. Perfect your invention, and give it a clever name.

Patent It!

Do you want to sell your invention? You will want to apply for a patent. Holding a patent to your invention means that no one else is allowed to make, use, or sell your invention in the United States without your  permission. It prevents others from making money off your idea. You will definitely need an adult to help you apply for a patent. It can be a complicated and expensive process. But if you think that people will want to buy your invention, it is well worth it. Good luck!

Ruth Wakefield's invention has become part of a favorite family tradition for many people.

1903 Ruth Graves is born in Easton, Massachusetts, on June 17.

1924 Ruth Graves graduates from Framingham Normal School on June 12.

1926 Ruth Graves and Kenneth Wakefield are married on June 26.

1930 Ruth and Kenneth Wakefield buy the Toll House Inn.

1933 Ruth Wakefield invents the Toll House Cookie.

1939 The Nestlé Company begins making chocolate chips.

1936 Ruth Wakefield publishes *Toll House Tried and True Recipes*.

1941–1945 The Toll House Inn sends cookies to the troops fighting World War II.

1966 Ruth and Kenneth Wakefield sell the Toll House Inn and retire.

1977 Ruth Graves Wakefield dies on January 10 at age 73.

1997 Chocolate chip cookies are made the official cookies of the State of Massachusetts on July 9.

antique—Something from the past.

biscotti—The name for cookie in Italy.

dietician—A person who is trained to plan balanced meals for both healthy and sick people.

hostess—A woman who serves food and greets people in a restaurant.

invent—To make or create something new.

menu—A list of foods to order at a restaurant.

nutrition—The process by which food is taken in and used by a living thing.

recipe—Directions and ingredients for making something to eat or drink.

Books

Jones, Charlotte. *Mistakes That Worked.* New York: Delacorte Books for Young Readers, 1994.

Priddy, Roger. *Make and Do Cook.* New York: St. Martin's Press, 2010.

Taylor, Barbara. *I Wonder Why Zippers Have Teeth and Other Questions About Inventions.* Boston: Kingfisher, 2003.

Thimmesh, Catherine. *Girls Think of Everything: Stories of Ingenious Inventions by Women.* New York: Houghton Mifflin Company, 2003.

Web Sites

Google Patents. <http://google.com/patents>

Famous Women Inventors. "Ruth Wakefield Chocolate Chip Cookie Inventor." <http://www.women-inventors.com/Ruth-Wakefield.asp>